The Next Step

Guiding you from idea to startup

Michael "Luni" Libes

Is this Book for You?

This book is a guide for inventors, innovators, students, and anyone else who has an idea for a product or service they would like to commercialize, but who needs some guidance on how to move forward from that idea to starting a company.

Steps, Questions, and Follow-up

This book is intended as a brief overview of the steps required to create a business plan and start a company. It is not an in-depth guide to each of these steps. Rather, along each step of this path, you will find targeted questions which will help you understand your own thoughts, needs, and desires. Take your time in answering these questions, using those answers to guide your decisions in getting from idea to startup company.

However, first things first. Read through the whole book. Note the questions as they come along, but do not spend time answering them. Focus instead on understanding the whole process. At the end of the book, you will find the full list of questions, and at that point you should have enough of a grasp of the process to start answering those questions. With those answers you can begin creating your company's business plan.

In this process, expect that an answer to one question may change the answer to an earlier question. Iteration is normal. In fact, when you have a complete set of answers, expect to go back and reiterate through all the answers at least three times, if not ten times – or in some cases, dozens of times.

Building a business plan is neither a simple nor a linear process.

Examples

To help demonstrate the lessons and provide model answers to the questions in subsequent chapters, I will provide two "real world" examples.

- "**Bird Watch**," a set of tiny radio "tags" used to measure wildlife behavior.
- "**Concrete Battery**," an energy storage technology using low-tech flywheels.

Bird Watch is based on a technology developed at the University of Washington. The researchers who created this technology wanted to create a product and company based on this work. In talking with them and other researchers like them, I found a common need. They needed help thinking through and creating their business plans. This book is partly the result of fulfilling that need.

Concrete Battery is one of my own ideas, which has yet to be implemented. Many of the inventors, students, and first-time entrepreneurs I meet hold on to their ideas tightly, sharing them with others only after signing non-disclosure contracts. I strongly advocate the opposite stance. I freely share my ideas with both people I know and people I have just met. As you are about to learn, the effort required to turn an idea into a company is far from trivial. The odds of someone stealing your idea are thus very low. The odds, however, of someone providing good feedback, introducing to you someone useful, pointing out an unknown competitor, or other serendipitous, helpful acts are quite high. That is why you should share.

These examples illustrate the process of starting a company. Regardless of what your own idea is, you can follow the process provided here to develop your idea into a company.

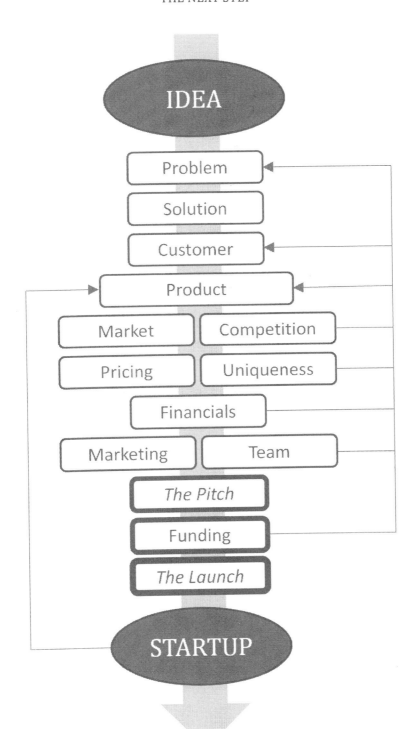

Table of Contents

1. Why?

Why are you going to all this trouble?

Before we begin, step back and answer some questions. What are the reasons you want to start a company? What are your goals? Do you seek financial independence? Career independence? Do you dream of seeing a few million people using your product? Or of seeing a few million dollars in sales? Have you always dreamed of starting a company?

> QUESTION 1:
> Do you (really) want to start a company?

A good way to help answer this question is to break it down into a series of forward looking questions, centered around what you expect your company and your job to look like five years from now.

> QUESTION 2:
> What do you expect your company to look like in 5 years?
> ($1 million, $10 million, or $100 million in sales? How many employees?)
>
> QUESTION 3:
> What do you personally want to be doing in 5 years? 3 years? 2 years? Next year?
> (CEO, CTO, sales, product development, advisor to the company, etc.)
>
> QUESTION 4:
> Are you prepared to quit your current job and work at the new company full-time?
>
> QUESTION 5:
> Do want to be rich, famous, both, or neither?

QUESTION 6:
At work, what makes you happy? Excited? Eager to start a new day?

The answers to these questions will help you decide whether you want to be an active part of the company you are creating, or keep to an advisory role. It will help determine the scale of the company to be built, and in turn the path and size of any fundraising. And with these answers, you should have sufficient information to decide the answer to question #1: whether to pursue this opportunity as a company at all.

2. Me, Myself, or Who?

You have an idea; that was the easy part.

My career began as a computer programmer. Within my first year out of college, I realized I was an entrepreneur, and before that year was up, at age 22, I started my first company. Over the past twenty years, I have founded and co-founded four other companies. And in that time I have filed two dozen patents, written over 30 business plans, advised more than 50 startups, and have taught Entrepreneurism at both the University of Washington and the Bainbridge Graduate Institute.

From experience I can assure you that turning your idea into a company is difficult. The process requires a tremendous amount of work, across a wide range of disciplines, many of which you likely have no prior experience. That said, this is a well-trodden path, followed thousands of times each year by people just like you, made possible by a network of service providers who can fill in much of the experience and labor that might otherwise present an impassible hurdle.

This process will take time. It will require a vast number of decisions. And it will often take multiple leaps of faith, demanding that you make these decisions with far too little information to know what is best.

Case in point: after deciding to move forward, your next decision is whether to get this company started on your own (with your current team, if you are not alone) or whether to search for a "business" person (i.e. someone with prior business experience or training) to join you as a co-founder.

> QUESTION 7:
> Do I start this company alone, or seek an experienced "business" person as co-founder?

At this point, before you have read this book and understood the process, many of you do not have anywhere near enough information to know the best answer to this question. The same is true of many of the questions posed in this book, when they are presented. If you feel stuck or unable to answer a question, skip it and come back later. Building a business is not a linear process. In fact, even when you do answer a question, you will likely have to revise that answer based on answers to later questions.

Back to the question at hand, even if you decide to seek a partner, it is still useful to answer all the questions in this book, as those answers will be at your disposal when your new partner asks you similar questions. If instead you decide to go forward on your own, the answers will guide your business plans. Thus either way, these questions are important to the process.

However, do not try to answer anything on the first read through the book. Read through the whole process first, *then* go back to the beginning and answer the questions.

3. Excitement & Passion

Your research, invention, idea, etc. is so exciting you can't sleep at night.

If you are not passionate about your idea, to the point of thinking about it in the half-asleep state each morning, in the shower, and five times per day, every day, then stop here. If you are not so excited about this invention that you bore your friends talking about it, then stop here. Stop, step back, and either continue refining your research until it does amaze and excite at least yourself, or hold back on your entrepreneurial dreams until you find something that does excite you.

> QUESTION 8:
> Are you passionate about your idea?

It is worth repeating here that starting a company is a long, difficult process. What makes people complete that process is the drive to see their product in the market, being sold to and used by satisfied customers. If you are not in love with your idea, odds are low you will make it through to see that goal fulfilled.

Thus, the answer to this question leads back once again to the answer for question #1.

Further Reading
The Monk and the Riddle by Randy Komisar

4. The Problem

If you have a solution in search of a problem, then you *have a problem.*

QUESTION 9:
What problem are you solving?

Consumers, in general, do not seek new product, service, or technology to buy. They seek solutions to their problems and are willing to pay money for solutions that work. What problem are you solving? How is the world a better place with your invention in the hands of your customers? Does it save people time? Does it save them money? Is it similar to an existing product, only much better? Is it a breakthrough invention, solving a problem that everyone has, but no one yet realizes is a problem?

To help demonstrate this and other topics, I provide two sample technologies: *Bird Watch* and *Concrete Battery*. For each of these technologies, I answer the question in the box above. For this chapter, the question is: "What problem are you solving?"

Bird Watch – [The problem] – It is time consuming and difficult to measure wildlife in the wild. Colored leg bands on birds' legs, and "chirping" radio tags on larger wildlife are the current state of the art. However, they provide only periodic glimpses of wildlife movements within a confined area and offer little opportunity to measure anything beyond a presence of a small sample of animals in a habitat.

Concrete Battery – [The problem] – Wind, solar, and other alternative energy sources do not produce the continuous and steady supply of electricity which customers demand. Batteries and high-tech flywheels are not cost effective at solving this problem.

Note that in the above examples, the initial focus is on the problem, not your solution, ensuring an understanding of the problem being solved. Next, as in these examples, it is good to start thinking about existing solutions to this problem. Further analysis of competition will also come later, but few problems exist that have no solution at all. Thus, in starting your company, you will have to think about not just solving your stated problem, but also how to displace the existing solution(s).

5. Whose Problem?

Problems do not buy solutions, people do.

> QUESTION 10:
> Who are the people whose problem you are solving?

Whether your solution is needed by individuals, companies, universities, or the government, some person will ultimately *decide* whether your product is worthwhile or not. It is imperative to understand who that person is, as they are your potential customer.

Who is this person? What is their role in their organization? Is this problem important to them? Do they know this problem exists? Do they already have a solution to this problem? If they want your product, do they have the authority and budget to buy your product?

Bird Watch – [Whose problem?] – Animal psychologists, wildlife conservationists, and others who research wildlife need a better/faster/cheaper solution for monitoring wildlife. Ranchers and farmers might have similar needs to track their livestock. Looking at tagging humans, retailers may have analogous problems tracking the behaviors of shoppers in their stores. Urban planners, too, might want to track the flow of people around cities.

Concrete Battery – [Whose problem?] – Wind and solar manufacturers would benefit from selling a more complete solution which provides a continuous and steady supply of electricity from their installations. The product managers at these companies would be the best people to talk to about this issue. Electricity providers may want to install centralized or distributed storage "farms" to balance the alternative energy production across their "smart" electric grids. The electrical grid designers and/or buyers of alternative energy at the electric companies would know if this is a problem.

In the case of Bird Watch, the animal psychology teams tend to be small, and thus it would be rather obvious who within those teams would know about the problem, and could provide you with feedback.

However, in the case of Concrete Battery, the two potential types of customers are actually very large organizations, and it would take further research to determine the organizational structures and associated job titles and roles of the people who would be aware of the problem.

Note that in these examples, only the people and problem are discussed, without even a hint of a solution. To best understand the opportunity, focus first on the problem and people involved. Once these are clear, you can return to your solution with confidence.

6. An Important Problem?

Your company can do well and do good at the same time.

The world is full of big, important problems. Most companies focus on two small problems: saving customers time, or saving customers money. Entertainment companies, on the other hand, focus on "killing" time while costing money. Meanwhile, few companies focus on improving the environment, lowering energy usage, minimizing waste, improving communities, expanding economic opportunities, or other shared problems.

> QUESTION 11:
> Are you solving an important problem?

Bird Watch – [An important problem?] – Deforestation and other human activities, along with climate change and other natural phenomenon are having an impact on wildlife and their habitat. Bird Watch can measure the impact on wildlife, and help us better understand the short-term and long-term implications of these changes.

Concrete Battery – [An important problem?] – Electricity consumption continues to rise year over year, continuing a century-long trend of increasing carbon emissions. Expansion of wind and solar electricity generation will help reduce the consumption of fossil fuels and eventually lower global carbon emissions. Concrete Battery's technology can help speed the adoption of wind, solar, and other alternative energy sources.

Your company does not have to be involved in environmental measurement or "clean-tech" to be helping solve important problems. For example, Starbucks provides an "affordable" luxury item, but while doing so, it promotes "fair trade" practices in its coffee bean procurement, serves its product in 100% recycled paper cups, and provides generous benefits to its part-time work force.

QUESTION 12:
Will your solution create more problems than it solves?

Every action you take with your company will have both planned and unintended consequences. Try to foresee as many of these as you can.

Sometimes, simple adjustments can drastically reduce any negative impacts, or greatly improve the benefits to your customers. For example, Starbucks' invention and use of the recycled cardboard sleeve keeps coffee warm, prevents the customers' hands from burning, and does so with minimal materials.

Think through every step of your business, from idea and product to distribution and disposal. Think though the environment you create for your employees. This is your opportunity to create a company from scratch, and with that, you get to decide how to do all of this "right."

Beyond Starbucks, take a look at Patagonia, Ben & Jerry's, Trader Joe's, Costco, and Netflix as model companies. While none of these companies directly solve the world's important problems, they do go out of their way to run their businesses in a conscientious manner, far above the norm.

7. Your Solution

With great problems come great solutions!

> QUESTION 13:
>
> Can you describe the problem and your solution in 10 minutes or less? Without a single word of jargon?

You have been working on this solution for years. It is complicated. It is subtle. It is a great technological breakthrough, or an incredibly brilliant idea. To get from idea to company, you need to be able to share the idea with others, mainly with people outside your area of expertise and with business-oriented, non-technical people.

In a later chapter, you will need to practice describing your product in under a minute. For now, work on a 10-minute summary. In those 10 minutes, describe the problem being solved, a high-level overview of your solution, and the types of people who will want to buy your product (or service).

In this process, throw away as much of the jargon as possible, ideally all of it. Create one or two diagrams which can be used within the 10 minutes to explain how the underlying solution works. But keep this at a high-level. Your goal is to explain the concepts to people who are outside your area of expertise. You will have plenty of opportunities to "go deep" into the details later, but at first you will likely have 10 minutes or less and thus no time for the details.

Bird Watch – [The solution] – It is time consuming and difficult to measure wildlife in the wild. Bird Watch is a technology solution which uses ultra-low powered radios, embedded into thumbnail-sized "tags," plus a set of battery-operated "base stations" which are deployed within the measurement area. The tags are small enough to be attached to the animals, and sufficiently low-cost so as to be disposable. The base stations are tied to trees or staked into the ground, and store the tag identifier and timestamp, along with the all data captured by the tags, whenever the tags get within range. Tags can monitor movement, temperature and pressure. As a system, the location and movement of a large number of wild animals can be monitored 24 hours per day, 7 days per week without the need of visiting the site more than twice (once to set up the base stations and tag the animals, and again at the end of the research period to collect the base stations).

Concrete Battery – [The solution] – Electricity consumers demand a continuous, steady supply of electricity. Alternative/green electricity technologies such as wind and solar provide a discontinuous, unsteady source of electricity. Concrete Battery provides a low-cost, flywheel-based solution to store excess electricity during times of excess generation, and to release the stored energy instantly when needed. The low-cost target is achieved by focusing on the mass of the flywheel rather than the velocity, foregoing the expense of high-technology solutions such as air bearings, vacuum containment, carbon fiber construction, and hardened steel enclosures. Instead, the Concrete Battery flywheels are constructed out of concrete, use off-the-shelf bearings, and are buried in the ground, using the ground as the containment vessel in case of "unintended deconstruction" (an important issue in flywheel storage).

Note the simplicity of both these descriptions. Both begin with a one-sentence restatement of the problem, then jump into the solution by describing the technologies. Note, too, some description of benefits (e.g. "monitored 24 hours per day, 7 days per week" and "low-cost").

These paragraphs sufficiently explain the gist of the solution at a very high, abstract level, without complicating the story with technical details, using little or no jargon, and without giving away any of the "secret sauce" which make these technologies patentable inventions. If turned into a slide presentation, each of these descriptions would be no more than five slides, including a diagram or two. Keep your descriptions just as simple.

8. The Buyer

The consumer and customer is not always the same person

> QUESTION 14:
> Who is the person responsible for buying your product?

Sometimes, the person with the authority and/or budget to buy your product is not the person with the problem. If so, then your sales effort will be more complex: first convince one person that your solution is worth having, then convince someone else that it is worth buying.

Bird Watch – [The buyer] – Animal psychologists and wildlife conservationists typically make their own decisions on the products and technologies they use.

Concrete Battery – [The buyer] – Both alternative energy manufacturers and electricity generating companies are large, complex organizations. The customer for Concrete Battery is most likely a Product Manager within those orgs, but any sale will likely go through a business development and/or procurement office, and depending on the scale of the sale, may also involve one or more executives.

Is your sales process going to be as straightforward as Bird Watch, or complex like Concrete Battery?

9. Your Product

The product of invention is an idea, not a sellable product.

Before you can start selling, you need to have a product or service packaged for sale. Is your solution ready for market as-is? Even if it successfully solved a problem you once personally had, it may not have the features needed to solve other peoples' problems.

> QUESTION 15:
> Do you have a minimal viable product (MVP)? What is the minimal set of features required to get the first few customers to buy your product?

Most inventors focus on the long-term vision of their idea, thinking about all the problems their product could solve, and the wide variety of people it can help. Being a visionary is great, but to get that invention into the market requires starting with the smallest initial step. The chance of long-term success is increased by launching the "minimal viable product" (MVP) as soon as possible, and from that point building toward your larger vision.

The minimal viable product is not the same as a prototype. A prototype is a product that contains a minimal set of features required *to prove that the invention works*. You may have already built a prototype to prove to yourself or others that your solution works as expected. Having such a prototype is great, as it greatly reduces the risk that the product will not work as promised. However, these features may not match the needs of your first customers.

A minimal viable product, by contrast, is the simplest possible version of your product that *someone finds sufficiently useful to buy*. So ask yourself: What is the minimal set of features required to get the first few customers to buy your product? You may in fact be past the minimum point today, or you may be missing one feature but have 100 extraneous features.

A common mistake is to hold off the launch of the product for "one more feature," worrying that you are missing something. Do not do this! If you do, you risk getting stuck in the process of development where each small addition seems a trivial amount of work, but which in the end postpones launching the MVP.

In postponing the launch, you are missing valuable information that you can gather only once the product is for sale. Before you launch, all you know are your own guesses of what customers need. After the launch of your MVP, you will have valuable information that can prove or disprove those guesses. Many potential customers will not buy your product, and from that you can learn of unmet needs. A few customers *will* buy your product. From them you can measure behaviors and with them discuss additional services. In both cases you learn far more about your market than is possible before the product is for sale.

> QUESTION 16:
> Are you ready to ship the product?

The pattern for success is simple: ship, measure, learn, adjust, ship, … More on this later. For now, the task at hand is to get the MVP defined, built, and in the market.

Bird Watch – [Is the product ready to ship?] – A few hundred tags have been built and deployed, along with a few dozen base stations. These were built in small-batches at commercial-grade. The cost to do that was exorbitant, but the product has been field-tested, and other institutions are now interested in this product. Thus, the current features seem to be at or above the MVP stage and the product is ready to go.

Concrete Battery – [Is the product ready to ship?] – This design is just on paper, and has never been built. The path to the market undoubtedly will require multiple trials. The MVP would be a handful of hand-built flywheels, capable in total of storing 25 kilowatt-hours of energy, and capable of storing and releasing that energy at a rate of at least 10 kW.

Talk to at least a half dozen potential customers, or better yet, a full dozen. Ensure the problem is important to them. Ensure the solution is viable. Then, and most importantly, use that information to determine the minimally acceptable feature set, and from there estimate the time required to get the MVP ready for market. Beware, however, of "paralysis via analysis." Instead of holding out until you know everything about your customers, remember that you will get better information after the launch.

> QUESTION 17:
> How long before the minimal viable product is ready for sale?

Further Reading
Lean Startup by Eric Reis

10. The Market

My product is so amazing; everyone who wants one, will buy two.

By now you have confirmed the problem exists, confirmed it is important to your customers, and you have talked to at least a half dozen potential customers. With that knowledge, plus research on the web, in libraries, or purchased from market research firms, you should be able to estimate how many people need a product like yours (a.k.a. the "target market").

> QUESTION 18:
> How many customers need your product?
>
> QUESTION 19:
> How many copies of your product will each customer buy?

Given the target market size, there are two methods for estimating the number of customers you expect will buy your product.

In a "top-down" model, you start with the target market size, then estimate the percentage of these people which will be your customers. This percentage (estimated customers divided by target market size) is called your "market share."

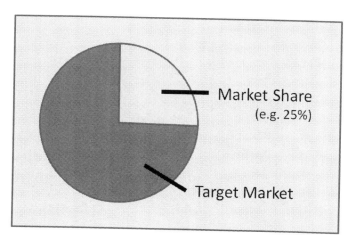

The alternative is a "bottom-up" model, in which you estimate the number of customers who will buy your product and how many copies they will buy. In this case, you can compute your resulting market share (estimated customers divided by the target market size).

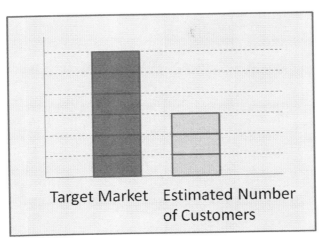

Target Market   Estimated Number of Customers

In both models, and in all the numbers in your plan, these are educated guesses, based on your market knowledge and above-mentioned research.

QUESTION 20:
What percentage of the market do you expect will buy your product?

QUESTION 21:
How many customers do you expect will buy your product?

Ideally, you have sufficient information to build both top-down and bottom-up models, and ideally the models will agree. If they do not agree, you can iterate through your assumptions to make them converge, or fall back on one model, using the other to justify its values. Usually, however, you will have only enough information to use one model or the other, not both.

No matter which model or models you use, repeat these calculations to estimate the market sizes for the first year and third year (and, if possible, each of the first five years).

Bird Watch – [Market size, Top-down model] – There are 80 active wildlife researchers in the United States. On average, each wildlife research project would require 100 tags and 20 base stations. (Note that this product has two components: tags and base stations). There are no equivalent products in the market today, and thus it is reasonable to assume 5% market share after 1 year and 50% market share after 3 years.

    After 1 year:
        80 researchers x 100 tags x 5% market share = 400 tags.
        80 researchers x 20 base stations x 5% share = 80 base stations.
    After 3 years:
        80 researchers x 100 tags x 50% market share = 4000 tags.
        80 researchers x 20 base stations x 50% share = 800 base stations.
    Total market need:
        80 researchers x 100 tags = 8,000 tags.
        80 researchers x 20 base stations = 1,600 base stations.

Concrete Battery – [Market size, Bottom-up model] – There are 50 wind and solar installations of significant size (more than 100KW) in the United States as of 2011. Starting with an unproven technology and unknown brand, a reasonable sales estimate would include 5 sales in year 1, averaging 2 flywheels per sale, growing to 15 sales in year 3, averaging 10 flywheels per sale.

    After 1 year: 5 customers x 2 flywheels= 10 flywheels.
    After 3 years: 15 customers x 10 flywheels = 150 flywheels.
    Total market need: 50 customers x 20 flywheels = 1,000 flywheels.

11. Pricing

100 @ $1/ea = 1 @ $100/ea

We need two definitions to help avoid misunderstandings in this chapter:

Price – The "price" of your product is the amount of money you ask your customers to pay you.

Cost – The "cost" is the amount of money it costs you to manufacture one copy of your product.

> QUESTION 22:
> High-price/high-service, small number of sales, *or*
> Low-price/low-service, large number of sales?

There are only two viable options for pricing. You can aim to be a high-price/high-service product. Or you can offer a low-cost/low-service product. "Service" here means the amount of time and effort your staff spends with each customer, including time both before and after the sale. In nearly all markets, it is not possible to successfully run a company in the middle (although in some markets, it is not possible to run a company at either extreme).

Bird Watch – [Pricing] – The goal is to make the tags as low-cost as possible, so they can be low-price. (The tags can solve problems outside of wildlife measurement, but are a viable solution for these additional markets only if they are inexpensive.) To start with, however, the tags will cost $10 each and the base stations $30 each, which means the prices will have to be somewhat high, for example $25 per tag and $150 per base station.

Concrete Battery – [Pricing] – While the Concrete Battery technology is touted as "low-tech" and "low-cost," this is only low relative to the competition. The goal is to produce the lowest-cost electricity storage solution, but Nonetheless, the initial installations will be priced at

$200,000 per flywheel, with a target price of $100,000 per flywheel after the first year or two. Thus, in regards to the answer to the question above, the Concrete Battery is considered to be a sale that is high-cost/high-service, and small in number.

Pricing affects the market sizing. If each Bird Watch tag were sold for only a dollar, the product, unchanged, would likely find far more customers in a variety of other markets, growing the total addressable market for the company. Similarly, if in launching the product, the actual price per tag wound up at $250 per tag and $1,000 per base station, the total addressable market might shrink. At that price the actual market may in fact shrink to zero.

Pricing can and should be based on the value to the customer, not on the cost of manufacturing. For Concrete Battery, the customers want to pay as little as possible, but the problem being solved costs those customers money today. Thus the solution only needs to be priced low enough to save the customers money as compared to other available solutions.

> QUESTION 23:
> What is the selling price of your minimal viable product?
>
> QUESTION 24:
> What is your target selling price of your beyond-minimal product?

The above examples are just two tiny tastes of the pricing questions. Many books have been written on pricing strategies. For now, a starting price and target price are sufficient.

Further Reading
Four Steps to an Epiphany by Steve Blank
Free by Chris Anderson

12. Opportunity Size

Is there a "there" there?

> QUESTION 25:
> How big is this opportunity?

Now that you understand the market size and have an initial set of prices, you can calculate the potential size of this opportunity. We do this by combining the answers from Chapters 10 and 11:

Market x Price = Opportunity

Bird Watch – [Opportunity size] – In Chapter 10 we determined that we could expect to sell 400 tags in the first year. In Chapter 11, we determined that the first tags would be sold for $25 each. That would mean we could expect to bring in 400 x $25, which is $10,000. We can expand this to the rest of the calculations:

After 1 year:	400 tags @ $25/ea = $10,000.
	80 base stations @ $150/ea = $12,000.
	Total = $22,000.
After 3 years:	4,000 tags @ $25/ea = $100,000.
	800 base stations@ $150/ea = $120,000.
	Total = $220,000.
Total opportunity size:	8,000 tags @ $25/ea = $200,000.
	1,600 base stations@ $150/ea = $240,000.
	Total = $440,000.

Concrete Battery – [Opportunity size] – In Chapter 10 we estimated that we could sell 10 flywheels in the first year. In Chapter 11, we set a price for the initial flywheels at $100,000 each.

After 1 year:	10 flywheels @ $200,000 = $2,000,000.

After 3 years: 150 flywheels @ $100,000 = $15,000,000.

Total opportunity size: 1,000 flywheels @ $100,000 =
$100,000,000.

QUESTION 26:

After reviewing the opportunity size, do you need to revisit the market sizing or pricing, or look for additional customers, or go all the way back and to the beginning and change the product?

Are you surprised by the vast difference in the sizes of these two opportunities? Before including the price, Bird Watch seemed to have had a lead, selling far more copies of the product to more customers. However, revenues (i.e. money earned by the company in selling the product) are what pay the company bills, and by far the larger potential revenues are found with Concrete Battery.

This highlights the difference between the two pricing models (i.e. low-price vs. high-price). Bird Watch is going to have to sell a lot of tags to be a viable business. Imagine how many tags it would need to sell if the price dropped to $10 or $1. Similarly, imagine (or calculate) how much revenue Concrete Battery would generate if it turns out they can continue selling their flywheels for $200,000 in year 3.

QUESTION 27:

Is the opportunity worth the effort?

---

13. Competition

With 7 billion neighbors, your invention is likely not unique.

> QUESTION 28:
> What other companies are solving the same problem?

It is rare to be the first company to solve a problem. While your solution may solve your problem in a unique manner, it is probably true that your potential customers are solving the problem today by some other means. The solution might be provided by a competitor, or may involve a manual process the customers have built on their own. In some cases the problem may be known but unsolved.

Before you launch your company, it is important to research the competition. Look at the features and pricing of those offerings. For solutions created by the customers themselves, calculate how much it costs them to implement their solution. For unsolved problems, calculate the cost to the customer of ignoring the problem.

> QUESTION 29:
> How does your product compare to the competition? How does it compare feature by feature?
>
> QUESTION 30:
> How does the price of your product compare to the competition? Which pricing model are they using (high-price/high-service or low-price/low-service)?

Displacing an existing solution is difficult. A rough rule of thumb is that your product needs to be at least 3 times (if not 10 times) better. "Better" meaning a combination of easier to use, faster to operate, and less expensive to buy.

This is true for both competitive products as well as for problems that go unsolved today. The latter may seem counter-intuitive at first, but realize that if the problem is not being addressed, it may be that the cost of buying or building a solution exceeds the cost of the problem.

Bird Watch – [Competition] – There are no other two-way radio-based tags for tracking wildlife, but there are other technologies used today. The tried-and-true method is to tag birds with colored leg bands and to tag other wildlife with leg bands or ear tags marked with serial numbers. Tagged birds can be spotted in the wild via binoculars while other animals are recaptured periodically and tracked using the unique serial number printed on the tag. In addition, animals can be tagged with broadcast-only radio-based tags, which periodically "ping" a signal that can be picked up by a researcher who is physically out in the field, and used to calculate the location (and no other information) of the animal. None of these solutions allow for 24/7, automated tracking, and none can collect information about the interactions between tagged animals. Lastly, the competing "RFID" technology also combines serial numbers with radio-based tags, but is incapable of measuring any data beyond "presence" of the animal near a base station.

Concrete Battery – [Competition] – A handful of companies solve the problem of electricity storage by using flywheels. All these solutions use high-tech, high-cost processes to maximize the energy storage in a minimal amount of space. By optimizing for volume, they do not optimize for overall cost. None of these competitors have sold many flywheels. In addition, many groups are researching electricity storage options, such as storage of compressed air, hydrogen generation, and batteries. None of these have more than a few trial customers, and none are on track to be a lower-cost option to Concrete Battery's solution.

When researching your competition, be fair and open-minded. These products have customers, and thus cannot be all bad. These companies made it into the market, and will exist after you follow suit. Focus not only on their weaknesses, but also on their strengths. Adjust your minimal viable product design (Chapter 9), pricing (Chapter 11) and estimated opportunity size (Chapters 10 and 12) accordingly.

14. Uniqueness

What is in your secret sauce?

> QUESTION 31:
> What is unique about your solution?

If your product is going to sell, it needs to stand out amongst the competition. If your company is going to thrive, it needs to make a lot of sales. What is unique about your solution?

The answer to this question will be important to share with people you recruit into your company, with investors, as well as with your potential customers. The details on how to make it work, however (the actual ingredients in your secret sauce) you should consider filing a patent (if possible), or keeping to yourself as a trade secret.

Bird Watch – [Uniqueness] – The core technology is an extremely low power radio, developed at the University of Washington's *Wireless Sensing Lab*. This radio allows the Bird Watch tags to be tiny and lightweight, and to be powered for weeks using an equally tiny battery. As part of their "secret sauce," the Bird Watch team has built upon this radio to create a "mesh network" to share data between tags, in addition to data uploaded to base stations. Plus, Bird Watch has added sensors to the tags, which allow a variety of data to be captured such as temperature and barometric pressure.

Concrete Battery – [Uniqueness] – In its current form, Concrete Battery has no "secret sauce." As the product is brought to market, the "secret sauce" will encompass the specific methods and techniques used to produce low-tech, low-cost flywheels.

Once you have documented the unique aspects of your solution, go back to your competition and do the same for their solution. If they have been in the market for years, there are no doubt features in your competition's product which are missing in your MVP. How important are these features to your customers? How long will it take you to catch up with any necessary features?

For Information on Patents
http://uspto.gov

15. Sustainable Competitive Advantage

Pull ahead and stay ahead of the competition...

> QUESTION 32:
> What is the long term, sustainable, competitive advantage?

This is a different question from the uniqueness of your solution or the current benefits to your customers. The previous two chapters ask about what is unique today and why customers should consider your product today. Now imagine that you have started your company and have launched your product. Your competitors will react and adjust. New competitors will arise. As you look out 3, 5, and 10 years, what will continue to be unique about your product and company that will help you attain critical mass and stay ahead of the competition?

Such advantages can be patentable inventions, or business partnerships, or low-cost processes, or simply being first in the market (a.k.a. "first-mover advantage"). In some markets, the largest provider gains a size and popularity advantage (a.k.a. "advantage of scale") which leads toward greater and greater market share (e.g. computer operation systems [Windows], web search [Google], trusted/loved national brands [Starbucks]). In other markets, the lowest priced competitor is the primary advantage (e.g. Walmart and Hyundai).

Bird Watch – [Competitive advantage] – The initial use of ultra-low-powered radios will allow Bird Watch to expand from tracking wildlife to other larger markets. Early experience in deploying products in that market will keep Bird Watch ahead of the competition as the uses of the product expand into other markets. In addition, these early sales should provide knowledge on lowering the cost of the tags and base stations, which in turn will lead toward greater sales and further decreases in cost due to scale. All of this can be summarized as "first mover advantage."

Concrete Battery – [Competitive advantage] – Having the lowest-cost solution will allow Concrete Battery to gain initial sales, and those sales will lead to a wave of press coverage. Patents will be filed on all key early learnings, protecting the long-term market by using "intellectual property" protection. And as the market grows in alternative energy production, Concrete Battery will be poised to grow along with it, as a proven, trusted, affordable brand for energy storage.

Further Reading

Competitive Advantage: Creating and Sustaining Superior Performance by Michael E. Porter

The Innovator's Dilemma by Clayton Christensen

16. Roles

You can't do it all alone.

> QUESTION 33:
> How many people do you need in your company?
>
> QUESTION 34:
> What is each person responsible for?

In a consulting firm, it is possible to have just one person. But in a company that ships a product (or service), there is simply too much for one person to do alone.

Someone needs to be responsible for:

- Specifying what the product does. (Product Management)
- Creating a shippable product. (Product Development)
- Selling the product. (Sales)
- Letting the customers know the product exists. (Marketing)
- Keeping track of the revenues, and paying the bills, including the payroll. (Finance)
- Ensuring everyone has a desk, a chair, a phone, that the government-required postings are on the wall, that the mail gets delivered, that the phone gets answers, etc. (Office Manager)
- Managing the team and making the final decisions. (CEO)

At a minimum, there are seven roles. That does not mean a company requires a minimum of seven people, as one person can fill multiple roles. It does mean that all these roles need to be assigned (as well as any others specific to your business), so that none of these responsibilities are overlooked.

> QUESTION 35:
> Who will develop your product?

QUESTION 36:
Who will sell your product?

QUESTION 37:
Who will market your product?

QUESTION 38:
Who will run the company?

Bird Watch – [The team] – Bird Watch is not yet up and running, and it has not yet recruited a full team. The initial team will likely include three people: a **CEO**, who is also product manager, finance, and office manager; a **technologist**, who focuses solely on product development; and one **salesperson,** who is responsible for both sales and marketing.

Concrete Battery – [The team] – Concrete Battery is also not operational, nor does it have a full team. Its initial team will likely include 7-10 people: a **CEO**, an **admin/office manager**, a part-time **finance person**, one person to do both **marketing** and **product management**, two **sales-people**, and 3-5 people in **product development**.

The larger team at Concrete Battery is due to the larger opportunity, the high-price/high-service model, the large size and complexity of the sales process, the complexity of making the technology into a product, and the customer support after each flywheel is sold.

It is easy to create a plan with a larger team, but such a plan requires more initial funding, more office space, and more time spent by the CEO in management tasks. It is better to pare down your plan to the minimum number of people, adding more only when necessary. Once your startup is up and running, is making sales, and is earning revenue, then growing a team will be easy.

Further Reading
Managing by Henry Mintzberg
Lean Startup by Eric Reis

17. Customer Benefits

Not just a want or a need, but a "must have!"

> QUESTION 39:
> What are the benefits of your product to the customer?

Your investors, recruits, and customers all need to know the benefits of your product from the customer's perspective. Do not leave it to the customer to figure out why your solution is of value to them. Spell it out in 3-5 clear, well-considered, potent reasons. As you create this list, keep in mind the benefits of your competitors' products, the uniqueness of your product, and your long-term competitive advantage. And do not lose sight of the problem you set out to solve. Do not list more than 5 benefits, since 3-5 is more memorable and impactful than 7 or 10 or 20.

Bird Watch – [Customer Benefits] – With Bird Watch, wildlife researchers can (a) accurately measure large numbers of animals; (b) measure a wide physical area; (c) measure more than just location, and (d) monitor animals 24 hours per day, 7 days per week with minimal human labor.

Concrete Battery – [Customer Benefits] – With a Concrete Battery flywheel, wind and solar manufacturers can finally sell systems which meet the expectations of their customers, providing a continuous, steady supply of power 24 hours per day, 7 days per week. With a Concrete Battery energy storage solution, electricity generating companies can efficiently add renewable energy to their supplies, storing excess production from wind and solar farms. Additionally, they can provide power instantly to meet unexpected demands.

These benefits need to all be positive reasons to buy your product, not arguments for why the competition's product is a worse choice. The benefits should "flow" from the earlier answers describing the problem, your solution, the uniqueness of your product, and especially from the customers' needs.

18. Marketing

If you build it... you need to do a lot before they come...

> QUESTION 40:
> How will your customers know your company exists? How will they know the benefits of your product?

So far so good. You have got a problem to solve, and a solution to solve it. You know who has that problem, and who at their organization will buy it. You have an estimate on how many you need to sell, and an initial price. You know the size of your team. You incorporate. You get the MVP ready for launch. Everything is ready. Exciting times!

Now, the next step is letting the world know your company exists, and, more specifically, getting your target customers to know your product exists to solve their problem.

Your salesperson should be someone knowledgeable about your potential customers, ideally with a list of contacts to call upon. It is far easier to sell to people who know you than to strangers, so do not hesitate to use your contacts as potential customers (a.k.a. "sales leads") and to ask them for additional leads.

However, that will go only so far. At some point, ideally before the product launches, you need to worry about informing the market of your product's existence, and create a plan of action to reach your target audience. You will need to announce the product on or soon after the launch date, and then on an ongoing basis. The goal of this effort is to put awareness of your brand and your product in the minds of potential customers, before your salespeople call them, to increase the likelihood that they buy your product.

Marketing is an enormous, complex subject, covered by thousands of books and taught to MBAs over multiple semesters. This is not something you will learn in a few pages. Instead, unless you plan on slowly bootstrapping your company, this is an area where you should consider hiring an experienced marketer. Depending on your product, this could be a salesperson who also is adept at marketing, or it may be a marketing specialist. In addition, even with the specialist, you will likely need some outsourced assistance, for things such as logo design, web site design, and public relations.

You will find a plethora of marketing consulting firms who are more than happy to work on your "brand," your "positioning," your "messaging," etc. But to start, you are likely better off spending more money to hire one person to do your marketing, rather than outsourcing the work to consultants. Ultimately, that decision depends on your specific market, the size and talents of your team, and your budget.

> QUESTION 41:
> What do you call this company?

One decision you need to make early on is the name of the company. You may have a name picked out now. However, you will need to ensure both that the name you have chosen can be trademarked and that the .com domain name is available (or a reasonable alternative). You can lookup trademarks online at the US PTO web site (www.uspto.gov/trademarks/). You can check domain names at the official InterNIC Whois registry (www.internic.net/whois.html).

Plus, in the age of the Internet, there is no excuse for not looking like a professional, well-funded company. Web sites such as 99designs (www.99designs.com) allow you to create a polished logo, web site, and printed materials at a minimal cost. And sites such as VistaPrint (www.vistaprint.com) can print your business cards, flyers, and other branded marketing materials.

Further Reading
Purple Cow: Transform Your Business by Being Remarkable by Seth Godin

19. The Elevator Pitch

You walk into an elevator and standing there is your top sales "prospect," the person your salesperson has been trying to talk to for months. You have 30 seconds before the elevator reaches the lobby. What do you say?

> QUESTION 42:
> Can you describe the problem and your solution in 1 minute? 30 seconds? 15 seconds?

You have been working on this solution for years. It is complicated. It is subtle. It is a great technological breakthrough. Nonetheless, if it solves an obvious problem, then it can be described in a pithy, 15-60 second summary.

This is a more important task than you might imagine.

This "elevator pitch" is the answer when people ask you, "What are you doing?" It is what you say when recruiting others to join your startup company. These are the words you use to start a potential sales conversation. And it is what you use in all initial conversations to get a loan, or a grant or to raise capital. We will return to the full sales pitch in Chapter 26, after you have developed your company more. But first we need a quick pitch to get the initial team on board.

Bird Watch – [Elevator pitch] – Bird Watch provides the best-in-class solution for measuring and tracking wildlife out in the wild, using a low-cost, low-power radio to capture a variety of sensor data, automatically... 24 hours per day, 7 days per week.

Concrete Battery – [Elevator pitch] – Concrete Battery turns the non-continuous electricity production of wind and solar installations into a continuous, on demand supply.

37

Congratulations, when you have completed your elevator pitch, you are now (slightly) experienced in marketing!

Further Reading

How to Get Your Point Across in 30 Seconds or Less by Milo O. Frank
Elevator Pitch Essentials by Chris O'Leary

20. Quick Financials

Grab a pen and the back of an envelope...

> QUESTION 43:
> Can this be a profitable venture?

Earlier in Chapters 10, 11 and 12, we did some rough calculations to decide if we could sell the product to enough people for enough money to make it worthwhile to even think about. Now we are ready to fine tune our initial estimates.

A full financial plan includes the expenses for everything per month, listed out for at least three years. Before embarking on that complex effort, we can first determine if this venture has a chance of profitability with a relatively quick, "back-of-the-envelope" financial plan.

Skipping past the initial growth phase, and using only your year 3 projections:

EXPENSES (money going out to run your business)

- List out all of the people you expect to hire, and each of their expected salaries
- Add 20% to this number to cover taxes and benefits
- List out all the other major expenses required to get the product ready for market, e.g. rent, licenses, patent filing fees, accounting, legal, public relations, etc.

REVENUES (money coming in from customers)

- Take the number of sales and the average price of each sale that you estimated in Chapter 12 ("Opportunity Size")
- Subtract the cost of making the product (a.k.a. "cost of sales") [Note 1: while it may seem odd to subtract the cost of sales from revenues instead of adding it to expenses, this is the common

practice]

[Note 2: for software the cost of sales is commonly $0, as the costs to development the product are considered research and development (a.k.a. "R&D") expenses, and generally only the inconsequential costs of duplication and distribution of the software are considered "cost of sales"]

Take the revenue number, subtract the total expenses, and see if you have a positive number. If not, go back through your financial assumptions and revise.

This simple exercise will help you understand whether you need to raise money or can bootstrap from your own savings. More importantly, if you cannot find a reasonable number of sales to offset a minimally-sized team, you have found a flaw in your business model.

If so, do not fret. It is not uncommon to have a good idea for a product, but no profitable path to bring that idea to market. Before giving up, step back, rethink your assumptions, and when re-planning, try thinking out-of-the-box.

Back-of-the-Envelope Financials

Formulas

REVENUES

Projected Revenues	R1	(Opportunity Size)
Cost of Sales	R2	
TOTAL REVENUES	R	R1 − R2

EXPENSES

Total Salaries	E1	
Estimated Taxes & Benefits	E2	E1*0.20
Total Other Expenses	E3	
TOTAL EXPENSES	E	E1 + E2 + E3

ESTIMATED PROFITS	P	R - E

Back-of-the-Envelope Financials **Bird Watch Example**		
REVENUES		
Projected Revenues 4,000 tags @ $25/ea = $100,000 800 base stations @ $150/ea = $120,000	R1	$220,000
Cost of Sales 4,000 tags @ $10/ea = $40,000 800 base stations @ $30/ea = $24,000	R2	$64,000
TOTAL REVENUES	R	$156,000
EXPENSES		
Total Salaries CEO @ $100,000 Technologist @ $80,000	E1	$180,000
Estimated Taxes & Benefits	E2	$36,000
Total Other Expenses Rent w/ Utilities @ $1,200/mo = $14,400 Legal @ $10,000 Accounting @ $2,400 Miscellaneous @ $1,000/mo = $12,000	E3	$68,000
TOTAL EXPENSES	E	$254,000
ESTIMATED PROFITS	P	$(98,800) not a profit, but a loss

The Bird Watch financials do not look promising. The estimated expenses are far higher than the projected revenues. In fact, the estimated revenues are not even sufficient to cover the salaries of the two employees. Shrinking the company to a single employee is not feasible, nor is halving the salaries.

Given this result, the next step is a step backwards, to return to the chapters on market sizing and pricing. More likely than not, that will be insufficient. Instead, this plan will probably need to be expanded into a new market, beyond tracking wildlife. If there is another market with a problem worth solving, which can be solved by the Bird Watch tags and base stations without little or no changes to the technology, and which would generate far more than $300,000 worth of revenues, then all hope is not lost for this plan. To see how this might work, see the "Example Plan: Bird Watch" chapter in the appendix, where one such alternative plan is explored.

"Pivoting" a plan into a new market or "pivoting" a product to solve a different problem is a very common practice when planning a startup. In fact, nearly all successful name-brand companies succeeded not on their original business plans, but with their second, third, or tenth revision of their plans. Companies like PayPal, Starbucks, and Coca-Cola.

Further Reading
Getting to Plan B, John Mullins and Randy Komisar
Plan B: How to Hatch a Second Plan That's Always Better Than Your First by David Murray

21. The Financial Plan

Rows, columns, cells, and formulae...

> QUESTION 44:
> How much capital is needed to break-even?

Once you have a back-of-the-envelope plan that is profitable (i.e. the revenues exceed the expenses), then the next step is a full-scale financial plan.

Fire up your favorite spreadsheet program. Row by row, list out all categories of expenses you can think of to run your business (e.g. salaries, rent, legal services, web site creation and operation, business cards, flyers, trade-shows, travel, telephone, internet, postage, etc.). Separately, list all the expected types of revenues (e.g. product sales, paid services, licensing, etc.). For the first year, fill out each of these expenses and revenues with one column per month. For each of the next two years, fill out each of these rows with one column per quarter (i.e. 3 month aggregate values). Grow your dream team as needed to keep up with the expected sales. Grow your expenses (e.g. rent) to keep up with the projected team size. Grow your revenues at a reasonable, believable rate, keeping in mind the size of your sales force and your spending on marketing. The end result of this is a massive spreadsheet with dozens of rows and at least 22 columns (row name + 12 months + 8 quarters + subtotals and totals).

Review and revise until both the expense and revenue projections look believable, based on the research you have done on your specific market. There is no guideline to these financials beyond being "believable."

Using these numbers, you will be able to compute the total amount of money you will spend before the company is "cash-flow profitable" (i.e. the monthly or quarterly revenues exceeds expenses). Add 20% to this number as a buffer for unexpected expenses, and that is the minimum amount of money you will need to raise to launch your company.

If at the end of the third year on your spreadsheet the revenues are still below the expenses, then continue reviewing and revising the numbers, or go back to revise the product to increase its value, or decrease the team size, or consider other options. Even if you have a profitable plan, continue revising your plan to minimize the expenses and maximize the likelihood of earning the projected revenues.

After at least a dozen revisions, if you still cannot make the numbers work out, you have a flaw, and may need to abandon the idea of starting this company. If this happens, do not fret. Put the plan aside for now, and look at it again in a year, or two, or three. Sometimes the flaw is in the "market timing," when a solution (especially a technology-based solution) is too early and too expensive to create a viable product or when an insufficient number of customers find value in your solution. Sometimes after a while a new technology comes along which makes the team size smaller or the sales process simpler, or something else happens that will lower the cost of sales sufficiently to make the financial plan profitable.

22. Risks

Life is full of risks, and so are startup companies.

> QUESTION 45:
> What are the risks of failure? What might go wrong? Which of your assumptions might be wrong?

What could go wrong in your plan? What stated or unstated assumptions might be wrong? How might your competitors adapt to your launch and eliminate your window of opportunity?

To paraphrase Helmuth Graf von Moltke's famous military quote: "*No business plan survives first contact with a customer.*" Or in other words, some of your assumptions are wrong, some of your decisions are wrong, and part of your plan is wrong. Which parts are right and which parts wrong are unknown. Nonetheless, to paraphrase another famous quote (this time from Winston Churchill), "*If you fail to plan, you plan to fail.*"

To get around the unknowns, take the time to think about the various risks within your plan, and as best you can, incorporate that knowledge back into the plan.

For example, there are risks in your financial plan: Can you get the product ready for market on the specific month listed in the plan? Will you really sign the first customer in that specified month? Will you receive payment from that customer in the expected timeframe?

All businesses have these risks. So, to offset these risks, create a version of the financial plan with an extra month (or two or three) accounting for these delays, and fund-raise and hire based on those numbers.

Similarly, no matter how conservative your estimated revenues may feel, there is a risk they are too high. Create a version of the financial plan with half of the expected revenues (either halve the number of expected customers or halve of the price or a combination), and consider what changes you would make if that were to occur.

23. Legalities

Surprisingly, sometimes you don't own your own thoughts...

QUESTION 46:

Do you own your idea? Do you have the legal rights to sell your idea/invention/research?

If you are a researcher at a university, it is likely that the university owns your research. If you are a salaried employee in the private sector, it may be that your current employer owns any ideas created on company time, or on company equipment, or related to the company product. In other cases, it may also be possible that you have signed away your inventions and ideas.

Before you make the effort to start your company, it is prudent to ensure that you have the legal rights to the ideas underlying your solution.

Check the paperwork you signed with your current and previous employers. If you find anything you do not clearly understand, have it checked by an employment lawyer (your lawyer, not your employer's attorney). And as you do this, read such agreements not only from your perspective, but also imagine how your employer might interpret the same agreement from their perspective. You may believe you are completely in the clear only to find your employer thinking you are stealing their "intellectual property."

If you do suspect that the concept is owned by your employer, the proper course of action is to negotiate a license, or if possible, to purchase the ownership of the invention. Payment for either of these options can be made with a percentage of ownership (a.k.a. equity), cash, or a percentage of future revenues.

Bird Watch – [Legalities] – The Bird Watch technology was developed at the University of Washington, paid for by federal grants. As such, the technology is owned by the university, and Bird Watch must obtain a license from the university before selling products based on this research.

Concrete Battery – [Legalities] – The Concrete Battery concept and preliminary research was created on my own time, on my own personal computer, and is unrelated to the areas of business of all my past employers. As such, I believe I am the sole owner of this idea.

In addition to licenses, you will need to incorporate your company. This can often be done on your own, but I highly recommend having it done by a lawyer, with additional advice sought from a tax accountant. The details of incorporation differ from state to state, and the number of options available continues to increase.

24. Fund-Raising?

It takes money to make money.

> QUESTION 47:
> Should you bootstrap your company or seek outside investors:
> friends and family, grants, incubators, Angels, or Venture
> Capital?

Do you have the cash (a.k.a. "capital") required to reach break-even without any outside investors? This process is known as "bootstrapping." If not, where will the money come from to start your company?

If you are a researcher at a university, what grants are available? If you are outside a university, are there grants available to you?

Do you have friends and family willing to invest in your startup?

Are there any business "incubators" or "accelerators" available within your business sector? (These two common terms refer to organizations which assist early-stage startups with space, mentoring, and sometimes small amounts of funding.)

If none of those options are open, then you will need to seek "professional investors," which take the form of "Angels" and Venture Capital funds (VCs). Angels are wealthy individuals, who invest their own money. Venture Capital funds are collections of wealth from multiple sources, managed by a group of professional investors. Note that VCs typically have a well-defined mission of funding companies in a specific industry (e.g. software, healthcare, clean technology, social enterprise) and often a specific stage of development (e.g. seed capital, early stage growth, later stage growth).

In terms of fund raising for technology companies, a good rule of thumb is that if you need less than $50,000, seek out friends and family, grants, small business loans, incubators, and if all else fails, credit cards. Between $50,000 and $1,000,000, seek out Angels, Angel groups, incubators, and the rare "seed-round" venture funds. Beyond $1 million, seek out "early-stage" VCs.

In all cases, the odds of finding the necessary funds are low. Which means the odds of getting your business funded are low (unless you use your own funds, which many people cannot do). I said this was not going to be easy! The odds of raising funds from Angels and VCs are often less than 1%. However, these odds can be increased. In the case of Angels and VCs, the investors choose their investments first and foremost based on the quality of the team, and secondly on the product. Which goes back to the question of team...

Further Reading
Venture Deals: Be Smarter Than Your Lawyer and Venture Capitalist by Brad Feld and Jason Mendelson

25. Recruiting a Team

It takes a great team to create a great company.

QUESTION 48:
Who do you need to recruit for your team?

Chapter 16 on "Roles" outlined the roles required to operate your company. You need to have at least three of those roles filled to increase your odds of fund raising above 0%, and to significantly raise your odds of successfully operating your company.

First, **you need a CEO**. Someone must be the full-time manager of the company. This person can also make sales calls, or do marketing, or the accounting, but this person cannot be a part-time CEO while working at another company. Investors need to feel confident that the CEO thinks about and manages the company every day.

Second, **you need someone to define the product**. Most often this is you. You did the research or you invented the invention, and with that effort, you defined the initial product concept. Someone now needs to be responsible for defining the minimal viable product (Chapter 9), and to manage the process of ensuring the actual product meets that specification.

Third, **you need someone developing the product**. This can initially be a part-time person, although to achieve outside funding, the investors will want to be reassured that this person is willing and capable of quitting their other job as soon as the investment is complete. For a software-based product, the product developer could initially be an outside consultant/contractor, but while some outsourcing is acceptable, it is important to have the head of product development as part of the core team.

The other roles can be filled after investments have been raised, or even after the company begins operations.

Recruiting a CEO, product manager, or product developer is itself a difficult process, full of risk for the future viability of your company. These are people whose work can make or break the company. Use all your resources to view as many candidates as possible. Do not settle on only people you know, nor the first person you find who says yes.

Nor should you assume that you will take one or more of these roles, just because you are a founder of the company. Instead, imagine that someone else started this company, and that you are being recruited to join the team. Which role(s) fit your prior experience? Which role(s) would you qualify to apply for in an interview?

That said, at the start, you (along with any partners) will need to fill every role yourself, but that is a temporary situation. As you create your plan, think about which roles you want to do yourself, and which you need to eventually recruit. Make sure these thoughts are included into your financial plan, created in Chapter 21.

Plus, as you think through that multi-year plan, think again about what role or roles you best provide for this company. As your company grows, think about which of those roles you are best at, and plan on hiring people to take those roles off your hands. Think about the size of team you are capable of managing. At some point in your plan, you may need to move aside and hire "scalable" management. Or in some cases, it may be best for you to move on altogether, and leave the company. Many first-time entrepreneurs believe their company cannot exist without them, only to find themselves being asked to leave. Do not fail to plan for this possibility.

The recruitment effort is an early bellwether of the success of your company. If you have difficulty finding someone to join your team and follow along with your vision, then future sales may be more difficult than you imagine, and the necessary expansion in your financial plan will be more difficult as well.

26. Creating a "Pitch"

Once you have a plan, everything from here on out is sales...

To recruit a team, you need a "pitch."

To raise money, you need a "pitch."

To sell your product, you need a "pitch."

These three pitches provide far more information than the "Elevator Pitch" you created in Chapter 19. The recruitment pitch explains why the product will sell and why the company is/will be a great place to work. The fund-raising pitch explains why the product will sell, why the team can execute, and how the company will make a profit. The sales pitch explains the benefits of the product to the customer, and how it will save them time or make them money or other reasons to buy the product.

Each of these pitches is a 10-15 slide presentation, presentable in 15-20 minutes.

These three presentations overlap in content, but are not identical. When creating each of these presentations, put yourself in the shoes of the audience member, and answer the questions they would have. Why should I work there? Why should I invest? Why should I buy? And remember the common theme: "What's in it for me?"

Two pieces of advice to remember when creating a pitch. First, wrap the pitch around a story. People like to hear a good story, far more than they like listening to a lecture. Tell the story from the perspective of an example customer. Tell about his or her need, and how your solution will improve that person's life. Second, entertain! Make the story interesting. Add suspense. Add humor. Make it memorable.

There are many books on creating a great pitch. The consensus calls for the following topics (with one slide per topic):

Investor Pitch	Recruiting Pitch	Sales Pitch
1. Problem	1. Problem	1. Company overview
2. Solution	2. Solution	2. Problem
3. Customers/ Market	3. Customers	3. Solution
4. Opportunity size	4. Market	4. Benefits to customers
5. Competition	5. Opportunity size	5. Price
6. Uniqueness	6. Benefits to customers	6. Uniqueness
7. Team	7. Uniqueness	7. Team
8. Financial Overview	8. Team	8. Q&A
9. Amount and planned use of funding	9. Financial overview	9. Next steps
10. Q&A	10. Q&A	10. Thank you
11. Next steps	11. Thank you	
12. Thank you		

For a step-by-step guide on creating and presenting your pitch, pick up a copy of the companion book, *The Next Step: A Guide to pitching your idea*.

Further Reading
The Art of the Start by Guy Kawasaki
The Next Step: A Guide to pitching your idea by Michael "Luni" Libes

27. Own the Room

Captivate, persuade, convince, and close.

Having a great pitch is not enough. You need to deliver that pitch in a persuasive manner. You need to grab the attention of the audience, making them feel as you do that the problem is important. You need to get them on the edge of their seats to hear your solution. And within the few minutes of the pitch, convince them that you and your team are the best people to deliver that solution to the market.

This is the talent of a good storyteller: the talent of captivating an audience. This is a talent you can improve by repetition and practice. However, beyond telling a good story, two other key ingredients are involved in delivering a great pitch: "own the room" and entertain.

When delivering your pitch, you need to "own the room," i.e. you need to command the attention of the audience, and keep in control of the conversation from the initial introduction through the answer of the final question. It is a good sign when the audience interrupts with questions, but you need to ensure you get through your whole pitch, and do not get side-tracked by questions of unimportant aspects of your plan. If needed, promise to answer that question later in the presentation, or in the "Q&A" (i.e. questions and answers) after the formal presentation.

In the Q&A, too often teams fail to deliver short, precise answers to questions. It is fine to answer with an "I don't know" or better yet, with an "I'll look into that," rather than making up an unconvincing answer on the spot. Remember, the Q&A is just as much part of your pitch as the opening slides. Before pitching, think about the likely follow-up questions, and if possible, prepare appendix slides with answers to those questions. Nothing shows preparedness better than flipping to a slide to answer a question.

Meanwhile, as you organize your pitch and work on "owning the room," do not forget to also entertain the audience. Show your passion. Smile. Act excited. Make your presentation memorable. Add humor to your pitch. Bring props. Get outside the box of one person standing and talking without interruption!

Investors, buyers, and recruits have seen pitches upon pitches. Few stand out as memorable. Everyone has a problem. Everyone has a solution. Everyone is faster, cheaper, or better than everyone else. To stand out from the crowd, you need to do more; you need to entertain.

In short, captivate your audience with a great story, keep control of the delivery of that story, and make it entertaining. Do that, and far more people will remember you, believe in you, and follow in your vision.

28. The Written Business Plan

Prose by any other name would read as sweet.

If you can skip writing out your business plan, by all means feel free to skip this step. In some circles, a presentation and financial plan together are sufficient for investors. However, for many Angel investors, for banks and many others, a written business plan is expected and required. A length of 10-20 pages is typical, including an Executive Summary of 2-5 pages.

The outline of the plan closely follows the investor pitch. In fact, some people write out the plan first, then summarize it into the pitch, while others start with the investor pitch and write out the script of the presentation as the text of the business plan. There is no one best way.

The key difference between the investor pitch and business plan is that you will not be present when the business plan is read. You will not have a chance to answer Q&A in person. Instead, you need to include answers to the most common questions in the plan, leaving less up to the imagination of the reader.

Business Plan	
1. Executive Summary	8. Team
2. Problem	9. Financial Overview
3. Solution	10. Amount and
4. Customers/	planned use of
Market	funding
5. Opportunity size	11. Reasons to invest
6. Competition	
7. Uniqueness /	
Competitive advantage	

29. Launch

5... 4... 3... 2... 1... Launch!

> QUESTION 49:
> Are you ready to launch?

You have the product, you know the market, you have recruited the team, and you have sufficient funds. Ready to launch?

The day you launch, the earth will not stand still. The sun will set as normal, and the front-page headline of the New York Times will not talk about your company.

If you are ahead of the curve, you will have a few early customers testing out your product, and your salesperson will have customers lined up to buy the product.

The key to operating a successful company is to get a product into the market that people will buy. That only begins when you launch the product, so as soon as possible, launch the product.

As discussed in Chapter 9, do not waste time perfecting the product. Do not add "just one more" feature which your product developer assures you will "take no time." Do not fret over one more conversation with a potential customer, or one more piece of research, to ensure your product exactly meets market needs. Launch the product. You will learn far more quickly once you are asking actual customers to pay real money for your product.

And most importantly, do not get caught in the common trap of thinking that the launch of the product is the end of the process. The first launch is the first step of the process of learning, optimizing, and as quickly as possible, re-launching an updated product.

30. Measure, Learn, and Update

Ship, measure, learn, adjust, ship...

> QUESTION 50:
> What are you measuring?
>
> QUESTION 51:
> What did you learn today?

You are not done planning when you launch the product. That is just the first launch of a repeating cycle of learning, updating and re-launching the product.

The key is to find a way to follow this pattern in as fast a cadence as possible, i.e. as often as can be reasonably managed. For successful web-based services, a typical cadence follows a weekly rhythm. Each and every week, the product is updated. Each and every day, the usage of the web site is measured, looking at day-to-day, week-to-week, and month-to-month trends. Each week, new features are added (or subtracted) or designs are changed. Each week, multiple experiments are run across 1% or 10% or 50% of the customers.

You likely see this in your own use of the web and mobile applications. Over the course of a year, your favorite web sites are noticeably changed in small increments every month or two. If you have a smartphone, you are likely barraged by application updates on almost a daily basis. And similarly on your PC, Firefox, Chrome, iTunes, Skype and other applications ask you to update to the latest version about every 6 weeks, if not more often.

> QUESTION 52:
> How often will you update the product?

For non-web based or non-app-based services, you still can and must measure your processes. How many new sales leads came in today?

What percentage of sales leads are viable candidates? What percentage of candidates buys the product? On average, how many phone calls and email messages occur before making a sale? What is the average weekly/monthly/quarterly sales price?

Measure everything you want to optimize, and keep asking questions about how you can improve.

Further Reading
Lean Startup by Eric Reis
Four Steps to an Epiphany by Steve Blank

31. Grow and Adapt

What works early on will not work forever...

Lastly, keep in mind that what works for your company when it is new will not necessarily (or likely) continue working as it grows.

As your sales increase, and your knowledge of the market increases, you will inevitably make adjustments to your product, to your marketing, and to your internal and external processes. As your team grows in size, you will at some point reach a scale where the ad hoc processes of an early-stage startup no longer function smoothly.

As your product achieves early sales success (should you be so lucky), you will eventually run into Geoffrey Moore's "chasm" where your product moves from the "early adopter" buyers to the "mainstream" buyers. Plus, around the same time you may have learned enough from the market to be ready to launch a second product, which ideally you will develop as thoroughly as you do the first product.

QUESTION 53:
Is it time to formalize your internal processes?

QUESTION 54:
Are you running out of "early adopter" buyers?

QUESTION 55:
Is it time for a second product?

In short, the lessons you learn in getting your initial product to market will be repeated over and again during the lifetime of this company you create. Keep learning, keep revising, keep adjusting, and adapt.

Further Reading

Crossing the Chasm by Geoffrey Moore

32. Review

You made it to the end! Nice job!

In a nutshell, you now know the basics of what you need to do to get your company up and running. Now that you have read through the process, it is time to go back through the questions, and start working on your answers. With those answers, start making decisions. With those decisions, put together your business plan.

You do not necessarily need to go through the questions in the order presented. In the process of fleshing out a business plan, you will inevitably hit road blocks and have to review your answers. Over the next few weeks, months, or years, you will change your mind, and revise your answers. In the process of researching the market, both before you launch, and after launch, you will discover new questions, whose answers will change how you answer other questions.

The important task at hand is to create a first-draft set of answers to the questions.

It is also important to realize that the plan you create today will be obsolete in a day or a week or a month. Periodically, you will need to go back to review and revise your plan. This includes revising your market analysis, your competitive analysis, your pricing, your hiring plan, and your financial plan. In short, everything listed in this book will need to be revisited as you get more information, including the answer to question #1 (revised slightly to: *Do you still want to start a company?*).

Now that you have seen the full list of tasks that need to be accomplished before and after launching, it may look daunting, but if you tackle a little bit at a time, a few questions every day, you will get through it all. With that, the next step is to execute that plan, and feel the satisfaction of seeing your vision realized in the market.

QUESTIONS

QUESTION 1:
Do you (really) want to start a company?

QUESTION 2:
What do you expect your company to look like in 5 years?
($1 million, $10 million, or $100 million in sales? How many employees?)

QUESTION 3:
What do you personally want to be doing in 5 years? 3 years? 2 years? Next year?
(CEO, CTO, sales, product development, advisor to the company, etc.)

QUESTION 4:
Are you prepared to quit your current job and work at the new company full-time?

QUESTION 5:
Do want to be rich, famous, both, or neither?

QUESTION 6:
At work, what makes you happy? Excited? Eager to start a new day?

QUESTION 7:
Do I start this company alone, or seek an experienced "business" person as co-founder?

QUESTION 8:
Are you passionate about your idea?

QUESTION 9:
What problem are you solving?

QUESTION 10:
Who are the people whose problem you are solving?

QUESTION 11:
Are you solving an important problem?

QUESTION 12:
Will your solution create more problems than it solves?

QUESTION 13:
Can you describe the problem and your solution in 10 minutes or less? Without a single word of jargon?

QUESTION 14:
Who is the person responsible for buying your product?

QUESTION 15:
Do you have a minimal viable product (MVP)? What is the minimal set of features required to get the first few customers to buy your product?

QUESTION 16:
Are you ready to ship the product?

QUESTION 17:
How long before the minimal viable product is ready for sale?

QUESTION 18:
How many customers need your product?

QUESTION 19:
How many copies of your product will each customer buy?

QUESTION 20:
What percentage of the market do you expect will buy your product?

QUESTION 21:
How many customers do you expect will buy your product?

QUESTION 22:
High-price/high-service, small number of sales, or
Low-price/low-service, large number of sales?

QUESTION 23:
What is the selling price of your minimal viable product?

QUESTION 24:
What is your target selling price of your beyond-minimal product?

QUESTION 25:
How big is this opportunity?

QUESTION 26:
After reviewing the opportunity size, do you need to revisit the market sizing or pricing, or look for additional customers, or go all the way back and to the beginning and change the product?

QUESTION 27:
Is the opportunity worth the effort?

QUESTION 28:
What other companies are solving the same problem?

QUESTION 29:
How does your product compare to the competition? How does it compare feature by feature?

QUESTION 30:
How does the price of your product compare to the competition? Which pricing model are they using (high-price/high-service or low-price/low-service)?

QUESTION 31:
What is unique about your solution?

QUESTION 32:
What is the long term, sustainable, competitive advantage?

QUESTION 33:
How many people do you need in your company?

QUESTION 34:
What is each person responsible for?

QUESTION 35:
Who will develop your product?

QUESTION 36:
Who will sell your product?

QUESTION 37:
Who will market your product?

QUESTION 38:
Who will run the company?

QUESTION 39:
What are the benefits of your product to the customer?

QUESTION 40:
How will your customers know your company exists? How will they know the benefits of your product?

QUESTION 41:
What do you call this company?

QUESTION 42:
Can you describe the problem and your solution in 1 minute? 30 seconds? 15 seconds?

QUESTION 43:
Can this be a profitable venture?

QUESTION 44:
How much capital is needed to break-even?

QUESTION 45:
What are the risks of failure? What might go wrong? Which of your assumptions might be wrong?

QUESTION 46:
Do you own your idea? Do you have the legal rights to sell your idea/invention/research?

QUESTION 47:
Should you bootstrap your company or seek outside investors: friends and family, grants, incubators, Angels, or Venture Capital?

QUESTION 48:
Who do you need to recruit for your team?

QUESTION 49:
Are you ready to launch?

QUESTION 50:
What are you measuring?

QUESTION 51:
What did you learn today?

QUESTION 52:
How often will you update the product?

QUESTION 53:
Is it time to formalize your internal processes?

QUESTION 54:
Are you running out of "early adopter" buyers?

QUESTION 55:
Is it time for a second product?

Example Plan: Bird Watch

[The problem] – It is time consuming and difficult to measure wildlife in the wild. Colored leg bands on birds' legs, and "chirping" radio tags on larger wildlife are the current state of the art. However, they provide only periodic glimpses of wildlife movements within a confined area and offer little opportunity to measure anything beyond a presence of a small sample of animals in a habitat.

[Whose problem?] – Animal psychologists, wildlife conservationists, and others who research wildlife need a better/faster/cheaper solution for monitoring wildlife. Ranchers and farmers might have similar needs to track their livestock. Looking at tagging humans, retailers may have analogous problems tracking the behaviors of shoppers in their stores. Urban planners, too, might want to track the flow of people around cities.

[An important problem?] – Deforestation and other human activities along with climate change and other natural phenomenon are having an impact on wildlife and their habitat. Bird Watch can measure the impact on wildlife, and help us better understand the short-term and long-term implications of these changes.

[The solution] – It is time consuming and difficult to measure wildlife in the wild. Bird Watch is a technology solution which uses ultra-low powered radios, embedded into thumbnail-sized "tags," plus a set of battery-operated "base stations" which are deployed within the measurement area. The tags are small enough to be attached to the animals, and sufficiently low-cost so as to be disposable. The base stations are tied to trees or staked into the ground, and store the tag identifier and timestamp, along with the all data captured by the tags, whenever the tags get within range. Tags can monitor movement, temperature and pressure. As a system, the location and movement of a large number of wild animals can be monitored 24 hours per day, 7 days per week without the need of visiting the site more than twice (once to set up the base stations and tag the animals, and again at the end of the research period to collect the base stations).

[The buyer] – Animal psychologists and wildlife conservationists typically make their own decisions on the products and technologies they use.

[Is the product ready to ship?] – A few hundred tags have been built and deployed, along with a few dozen base stations. These were built in small-batches at commercial-grade. The cost to do that was exorbitant, but the product has been field-tested, and other institutions are now interested in this product. Thus, the current features seem to be at or above the MVP stage and the product is ready to go.

[Market size, Top-down model] – There are 80 active wildlife researchers in the United States. On average, each wildlife research project would require 100 tags and 20 base stations. (Note that this product has two components: tags and base stations). There are no equivalent products in the market today, and thus it is reasonable to assume 5% market share after 1 year and 50% market share after 3 years.

After 1 year:
    80 researchers x 100 tags x 5% market share = 400 tags.
    80 researchers x 20 base stations x 5% share = 80 base stations.

After 3 years:
    80 researchers x 100 tags x 50% market share = 4000 tags.
    80 researchers x 20 base stations x 50% share = 800 base stations.

Total market need:
    80 researchers x 100 tags = 8,000 tags.
    80 researchers x 20 base stations = 1,600 base stations.

[Pricing] – The goal is to make the tags as low-cost as possible, so they can be low-price. (The tags can solve problems outside of wildlife measurement, but are a viable solution for these additional markets only if they are inexpensive.) To start with, however, the tags will cost $10 each and the base stations $30 each, which means the prices will have to be somewhat high, for example $25 per tag and $150 per base station.

[Opportunity size] – In Chapter 10 we determined that we could expect to sell 400 tags in the first year. In Chapter 11, we determined that the first tags would be sold for $25 each. That would mean we could expect to bring in 400 x $25, which is $10,000. We can expand this to the rest of the calculations:

After 1 year:	400 tags @ $25/ea = $10,000. 80 base stations @ $150/ea = $12,000. Total = $22,000.
After 3 years:	4,000 tags @ $25/ea = $100,000. 800 base stations@ $150/ea = $120,000. Total = $220,000.
Total opportunity size:	8,000 tags @ $25/ea = $200,000. 1,600 base stations@ $150/ea = $240,000. Total = $440,000.

[Competition] – There are no other two-way radio-based tags for tracking wildlife, but there are other technologies used today. The tried-and-true method is to tag birds with colored leg bands and to tag other wildlife with leg bands or ear tags marked with serial numbers. Tagged birds can be spotted in the wild via binoculars while other animals are recaptured periodically and tracked using the unique serial number printed on the tag. In addition, animals can be tagged with broadcast-only radio-based tags, which periodically "ping" a signal that can be picked up by a researcher who is physically out in the field, and used to calculate the location (and no other information) of the animal. None of these solutions allow for 24/7, automated tracking, and none can collect information about the interactions between tagged animals. Lastly, the competing "RFID" technology also combines serial numbers with radio-based tags, but is incapable of measuring any data beyond "presence" of the animal near a base station.

[Uniqueness] – The core technology is an extremely low power radio, developed at the University of Washington's *Wireless Sensing Lab*. This radio allows the Bird Watch tags to be tiny and lightweight, and to be powered for weeks using an equally tiny battery. As part of their "secret sauce," the Bird Watch team has built upon this radio to create a "mesh network" to share data between tags, in addition to data uploaded to base stations. Plus, Bird Watch has added sensors to the tags, which allow a variety of data to be captured such as temperature and barometric pressure.

[Competitive advantage] – The initial use of ultra-low-powered radios will allow Bird Watch to expand from tracking wildlife to other larger markets. Early experience in deploying products in that market will keep Bird Watch ahead of the competition as the uses of the product expand into other markets. In addition, these early sales should provide knowledge on lowering the cost of the tags and base stations, which in turn will lead toward greater sales and further decreases in cost due to scale.

[The team] – Bird Watch is not yet up and running, and it has not yet recruited a full team. The initial team will likely include three people: a **CEO**, who is also product manager, finance, and office manager; a **technologist**, who focuses solely on product development; and one **salesperson,** who is responsible for both sales and marketing.

[Customer Benefits] – With Bird Watch, wildlife researchers can (a) accurately measure large numbers of animals; (b) measure a wide physical area; (c) measure more than just location, and (d) monitor animals 24 hours per day, 7 days per week with minimal human labor.

[Elevator pitch] – Bird Watch provides the best-in-class solution for measuring and tracking wildlife out in the wild, using a low-cost, low-power radio to capture a variety of sensor data, automatically... 24 hours per day, 7 days per week.

[Back-of-the-envelope financials] —

Back-of-the-Envelope Financials Bird Watch Example		
REVENUES		
Projected Revenues 4,000 tags @ $25/ea = $100,000 800 base stations @ $150/ea = $120,000	R1	$220,000
Cost of Sales 4,000 tags @ $10/ea = $40,000 800 base stations @ $30/ea = $24,000	R2	$64,000
TOTAL REVENUES	R	$156,000
EXPENSES		
Total Salaries CEO @ $100,000 Technologist @ $80,000	E1	$180,000
Estimated Taxes & Benefits	E2	$36,000
Total Other Expenses Rent w/ Utilities @ $1,200/mo = $14,400 Legal @ $10,000 Accounting @ $2,400 Miscellaneous @ $1,000/mo = $12,000	E3	$68,000
TOTAL EXPENSES	E	$254,000
ESTIMATED PROFITS	P	$(98,800) not a profit, but a loss

[Legalities] — The Bird Watch technology was developed at the University of Washington, paid for by federal grants. As such, the technology is owned by the university, and Bird Watch must obtain a license from the university before selling products based on this research.

Critique: Oh dear, the back-of-the-envelope says this company, with the estimated revenues from year 3, is not profitable. This, despite the team only consisting of two people (noting I removed the sales person from the original estimated team), and with a very lean set of expenses.

If your plan has the same flaw, there are a few options for trying to fit it. And even if your plan is profitable, it is often worth the effort to iterate and revise your plan. First, go back to the market in Chapter 10. Are there other potential customers with similar problems in unrelated markets? Second, go back to the pricing in Chapter 11. Will the customers pay more than you estimated? Third, is your "cost of sales" as low as possible? In the Bird Watch example above, the tags cost the company $10 each. Is there any alternative technology that could drop that to $5? What would it take to drop the cost to $1?

If after all these iterations, the plan is still not profitable, or if the only way to get to profitability is to push the assumptions so far as to be unbelievable (e.g. 90% of potential customers will buy your product), then the plan is truly flawed and it should not be pursued until something significant changes to make it potentially profitable.

Rather than giving up on this plan, let's go all the way back to the problem, "pivot" the Bird Watch solution to focus on a different market, and see what happens:

[The problem – pivot] – In the process of raising chickens, turkeys, ducks and other poultry on modern farms, a significant number of birds die before reaching maturity. It is time consuming and difficult for poultry farmers to measure the living conditions of their birds, to determine the cause of these deaths.

[Whose problem? – pivot] – Poultry farmers lose money when their birds die before they are ready to be sold at market.

[An important problem? – pivot] – Birds are unnecessarily suffering on today's modern poultry farms. Improving the quality of these animals' lives is very much a worthwhile goal.

[The solution – pivot] – It is time consuming and difficult to measure the living conditions of birds on a poultry farm. Bird Watch is a technology-based solution which uses ultra-low powered radios, embedded into thumbnail-sized "tags," plus a set of battery-operated "base stations" which are deployed every 100-1,000 square meters within the measurement area. The tags are small enough to be attached to the animals, and sufficiently low-cost to be disposable, although expensive enough that only a small portion of the birds within a flock would be tagged. The base stations are also battery operated, easily disbursed around the barn and elsewhere around the farm. When a tag comes within range of a base station the tag identifier and timestamp is transferred to the base station, along with other data captured by the tags. Tags can monitor movement, temperature , pressure, sound levels, and light levels. As a system, once the birds are tagged and the base stations installed, the location and movement of the tagged birds can be monitored on a 24/7 basis without human involvement.

[The buyer – pivot] – The people choosing to buy the Bird Watch system are likely the owners of the poultry farms, who have a strong financial interest in minimizing premature animal deaths on their farms.

[Is the product ready to ship? – pivot] – While Bird Watch has been tested in the field by animal psychologists measuring wild birds, it has not been used by poultry farmers measuring domesticated birds. There are very likely minor changes required to meet the needs of these new customers.

[Market size, Top-down model – pivot] – According to the United States Department of Agriculture (USDA), in 1995 there were 49,716 poultry farms in the United States. In 2010, 8.3 billion chickens and 244 million turkeys were raised in the United States. Of those animals, 107 million chickens died prematurely, plus an unreported number of turkeys. If Bird Watch were used to measure just 0.001% of the total birds, 85,440 tags per year would be required. If 10 base stations were installed on just 2% of those farms, 9,940 base stations would be required.

[Market size, Bottom-up model – pivot] – Without further market research, the expected market share of Bird Watch in the poultry farming market can not accurately be estimated. To help justify the above model, it is useful to create a bottom-up market size estimate.

After 1 year:
    25 farms x 100 tags = 2,500 tags.
    25 farms x 10 base stations = 250 base stations.

After 3 years:
    1,000 farms x 100 tags = 100,000 tags.
    1,000 farms x 10 base stations = 10,000 base stations.

Total market need:
    50,000 farms x 1000 tags = 50,000,000 tags.
    50,000 farms x 50 base stations = 2,500,000 base stations.

Nicely, the top-down and bottom-up models for year 3 are sufficiently close to believe that these estimates are reasonable first draft values. Further customer discussions and other market research are needed to validate these estimates further.

[Pricing – pivot] – The goal is to make the tags as low-price as possible. In year one, the tags will be priced at $25 each and the base stations $150 each. By year 3 the goal is to price the tags at $10 each and the base stations at $100 each, with a cost of $5 and $25 respectively. At full scale, the tags should be priced at no more than $5, and the base stations can continue to be priced at $100.

[Opportunity size – pivot] – Multiplying the market size by the pricing:

After 1 year:
    2,500 tags x $25/ea = $62,500.
    250 base stations x $150/ea = $37,500.
    Total = $100,000.

After 3 years:
    100,000 tags x $10/ea = $1,000,000.

10,000 base stations x $100/ea = $1,000,000.
Total = $2,000,000.

Total opportunity size:
50,000,000 tags x $5/ea = $ 250,000,000.
2,500,000 base stations x $100/ea = $ 250,000,000.
Total = $500,000,000.

[Competition – pivot] – There are no other two-way radio-based tags for tracking poultry on poultry farms. Rather than monitoring the birds, today's poultry farms monitor the barns housing the birds.

[Uniqueness – pivot] – The uniqueness of the Bird Watch does not change along with the switch from tracking wildlife to tracking poultry. The core technology is an extremely low power radio, which allows the Bird Watch tags to be tiny, lightweight, and powered for weeks; combined into a "mesh network" to share data between tags and base stations; and to capture a variety of data.

[Competitive advantage – pivot] – The existing systems for minimizing the death of birds at poultry farms is failing to prevent over 107 million animal deaths. If Bird Watch can save even only a few percentage of these animals, the farmers will earn sufficient revenues to pay for the Bird Watch tags, plus an additional profit. Once proven to "pay for itself," farmers will be reluctant to stop using Bird Watch, risking the loss of those savings. Any competitive product would need to prove greater savings before a customer would bother to test it out.

[The team – pivot] – No new team members are required in shifting the focus of Bird Watch from tracking wildlife to tracking poultry. The initial team will likely include three people: a CEO, a technologist, and one salesperson.

[Customer Benefits – pivot] – With Bird Watch, poultry farmers can (a) better understand the causes of premature animal deaths; (b) reduce the number of these deaths; and in turn (c) increase the overall health of the poultry flock, and (d) earn additional income by bringing a greater number of birds to maturity.

[Elevator pitch – pivot] – Bird Watch helps poultry farmers maximize the health and well being of their birds, using a low-cost, low-power radio tag to monitor their flock, automatically... 24 hours per day, 7 days per week.

Back-of-the-Envelope Financials **Bird Watch Example**		
REVENUES		
Projected Revenues 100,000 tags @ $10/ea = $1,000,000 10,000 base stations @ $100/ea = $1,000,000	R1	$2,000,000
Cost of Sales 100,000 tags @ $5/ea = $500,000 10,000 base stations @ $25/ea = $250,000	R2	$750,000
TOTAL REVENUES	R	$1,250,000
EXPENSES		
Total Salaries CEO @ $100,000 Technologist @ $80,000 Sales @ $120,000	E1	$300,000
Estimated Taxes & Benefits	E2	$60,000
Total Other Expenses Rent w/ Utilities @ $1,200/mo = $14,400 Legal @ $10,000 Accounting @ $2,400 Miscellaneous @ $1,000/mo = $12,000	E3	$68,000
TOTAL EXPENSES	E	$428,000
ESTIMATED PROFITS	P	$750,000

Critique: The Bird Watch financials in this iteration show a profit! And there is a sufficient profit that in the more detailed financial plan, additional team members could be added, the price of the tags adjusted, or other necessary adjustments made.

The point of the back-of-the-envelope financials is simply to show that the business might be profitable, and the above table does that quite well. Well enough that this plan seems reasonable to move forward into details financials and the remainder of the business planning process.

Acknowledgements

Thank you to the staff and Entrepreneurs in Residence at the University of Washington's Center for Commercialization (http://depts.washington.edu/uwc4c) for their feedback. Similarly to the researchers at Encounternet and other researchers at the University of Washington whose entrepreneurial passions led me to begin writing this book.

Thank you to Gifford Pinchot III, President and Co-founder of the Bainbridge Graduate Institute (http://bgi.edu) for his foresight into the future of entrepreneurship, and his openness to my mind's wanderings.

Thank you to Michele Morgan (VP at BGI) for her help in editing, fit within the busy 50 hours of *#SocEnt Weekend* (http://socentweekend.org).

And most of all, thanks to Monica Aufrecht, who relentlessly ensured my words matched my thoughts, and that those words would be understandable to you without the aid of a business school education or a business jargon dictionary.

About the Author

Michael "Luni" Libes is a 20+ year serial entrepreneur, most recently founding Fledge LLC, the "conscious company" incubator. Fledge helps create and accelerate companies meeting the needs of the large and growing number of consumers who are: environmentally conscious, energy conscious, health conscious, conscious of sustainability, of community, and even conscious of consumption itself.
http://fledge.co *@FledgeLLC*

Luni is an Entrepreneur in Residence and Entrepreneurship Instructor at the Bainbridge Graduate Institute, advisor to The HUB Seattle, to SURF Incubator, and to a dozen startup companies. He is also an Entrepreneur in Residence Emeritus for the University of Washington's Center for Commercialization
http://bgi.edu   *http://depts.washington.edu/uwc4c/*
http://thehubseattle.com   *http://surfincubator.com*

Luni is a co-creator and organizer of *#SocEnt Weekend*, a hands-on, action-based, high-energy, 50 hour weekend event for teaching social entrepreneurship and creating impactful companies.
http://socentweekend.org *@SocEntWeekend*

Luni began his 20+ year career in software, founding and co-founding four startups and joining a fifth. These include: Ground Truth (mobile market research and analysis), Medio Systems (mobile search and advertising), Mforma (mobile gaming and applications), 2WAY (enterprise collaboration systems), and Nimble (pen computing, PDAs, and early smartphones).

Further Reading

The Next Step: A guide to pitching your idea by Michael "Luni" Libes

The Art of the Start by Guy Kawasaki

Business Model Generation by Alexander Osterwalder & Yves Pigneur

Competitive Advantage: Creating and Sustaining Superior Performance by Michael E. Porter

Crossing the Chasm by Geoffrey Moore

The Dip: A Little Book That Teaches You When to Quit (and When to Stick) by Seth Godin

Elevator Pitch Essentials by Chris O'Leary

Evil Plans by Hugh MacLeod

Four Steps to an Epiphany by Steve Blank

Free by Chris Anderson

Getting to Plan B, John Mullins and Randy Komisar

How to Get Your Point Across in 30 Seconds or Less by Milo O. Frank

The Innovator's Dilemma by Clayton Christensen

Lean Startup by Eric Reis

Managing by Henry Mintzberg

The Monk and the Riddle by Randy Komisar

Plan B: How to Hatch a Second Plan That's Always Better Than Your First by David Murray

Purple Cow: Transform Your Business by Being Remarkable by Seth Godin

Venture Deals: Be Smarter Than Your Lawyer and Venture Capitalist by Brad Feld and Jason Mendelson

For Information on Patents

http://uspto.gov

Index

17940382R00051

Made in the USA
Charleston, SC
08 March 2013